The Itchy Dingo

WRITTEN BY PATRICK STEINEMANN
ILLUSTRATED BY MICHAEL CONNOLLY

This book acknowledges the Footprints of the Ancestors as the original copyrights of Australia and First Australians as the protectors of their Original Creation.

This story is written to honor Aboriginal Australians. If genuine originality means to be true to one's origins, these one hundred percent Original men and women have been true to theirs since the dawn of the Dreamtime.

Illustrations by Michael Connolly

Aboriginal names used courtesy of kullillaart.com.au

Under the cloudless sky of the Australian outback lived a dingo[1] named Taj.[2]

He was a restless fellow with a skin problem that made him scratch nonstop. The more Taj scratched, the more it itched. The more it itched, the more he scratched until he could not stand it any longer.

"Something must be wrong with this place! I've got to get out of here before my itching gets worse!"

Not beating around the bush, Taj packed up a few belongings and his favorite pillow and went looking for a place where he could get rid of his itch.

On the advice of his fellow dingoes, Taj went to seek the counsel of Mulga, the king brown snake.[3] He found his highness curled up under a rock.

Being a king, Mulga had a high opinion of himself. He saw everyone as a subject who should crawl at his feet—except he didn't have any feet.

Carefully approaching the snake, Taj asked respectfully, "Your Majesty, do you know a cure for itching?"

Mulga hissed in reply, "Lie flat on your belly. The hotter the ground, the better."

Taking Mulga's advice, Taj laid down on the hot red sand and did not move from that position all day, thereby scorching his stomach. Coupled with his constant scratching, his body was now racked with pain.

Next, he met Bohra, a giant red kangaroo.[4] While scratching himself, Taj explained his affliction.

"Jump around," suggested Bohra. "The bounce will take the itch out of you."

Taj did as he was told, and between bouts of scratching, he jumped and jumped until he had no spring left.

Still wobbly from all the jumping, he bumped into a koala[5] named Koobor. Roused from his reverie, Koobor took some gum leaves from his front pouch and offered them to Taj.

"Chew them and you will feel sooooo gooood. It will make you snoooooze and dream your life away and help you forget about itching."

Taking the koala's advice, Taj ate nothing but eucalyptus leaves for many days and soon found himself in a strange kind of daze.

Still, even in this dream-like haze, his itching didn't go away. He nearly scratched out the last of his fur when he was saved by the cacophony of the galahs, parrots, lorikeets, and cockatoos that woke him not a moment too soon.

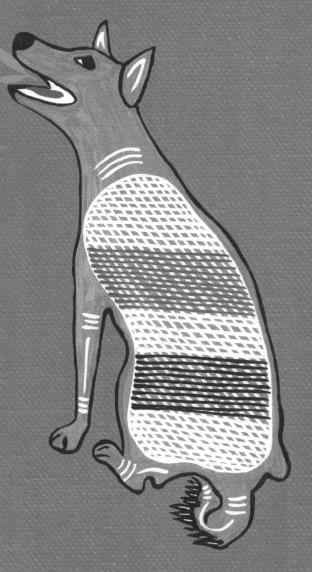

Nothing seemed to be working and Taj was about to go out of his mind. One moment he stood. The next, he ran. He jumped up, he laid down. He shook his head furiously and clawed at the ground.

All of this was noticed by Goo-Goor-Gaga, the kookaburra,[6] who started to laugh at him. "You wouldn't think it's so funny if you knew how miserable I am," Taj cried out pitifully.

"Don't take things too seriously," replied Goo-Goor-Gaga. "What you need is to laugh it off."

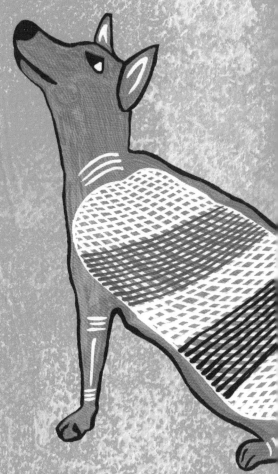

Since dingoes don't know much about laughing, Taj did the next best thing and howled at the moon. All night long, the sound of his howling echoed throughout the desert. When morning came, his voice had become so hoarse that he could barely pant while scratching himself.

All this left Taj itching for a drink. He went to a nearby waterhole, where he met an odd creature with webbed feet and a flat nose like a duck.

Taj could not help but ask in a whisper since he had nearly lost his voice from howling, "What is wrong with you? Are you okay? Did someone squash your nose?"

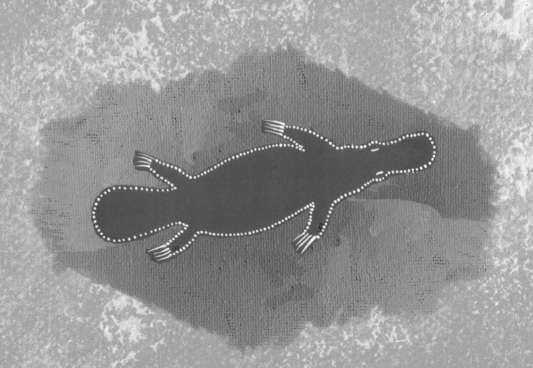

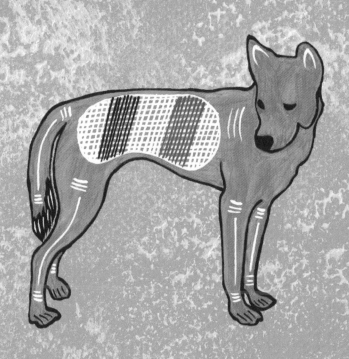

"Look who's talking," retorted the ill-tempered billed animal, who turned out to be a platypus[7] named Gaya-Dari.

Being touchy about his looks, he scolded Taj. "You are one to ask! You are scrawny and dirty. Your skin is all burnt, and you stink. What you need is a bath!"

"Now, why didn't I think of that sooner?" thought Taj. "The cool, fresh water will soothe my skin."

But as he jumped in the water, he was seized by such a violent urge to scratch that he forgot all about swimming and nearly drowned.

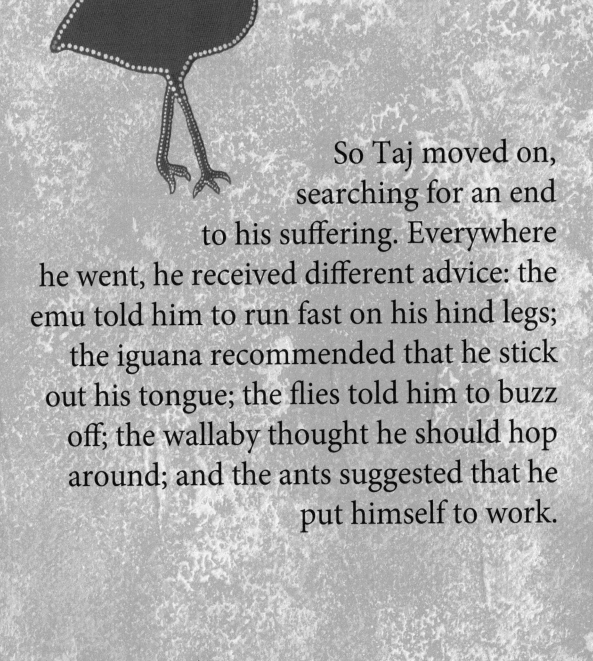

So Taj moved on, searching for an end to his suffering. Everywhere he went, he received different advice: the emu told him to run fast on his hind legs; the iguana recommended that he stick out his tongue; the flies told him to buzz off; the wallaby thought he should hop around; and the ants suggested that he put himself to work.

Taj tried everything, but nothing worked. Instead, his itching only grew worse.

Finally, he came to a billabong,[8] where he found a group of animals gathered for a drink. On hearing Taj's plea for help, they decided to hold a council to discuss his case.

The thorny dragon[9] acknowledged that Taj's problem was a thorny one. The possum thought he should play possum.[10] The crocodile snapped that Taj should toughen up by getting thicker skin. The fruit bats, dangling from the tree branches above, encouraged him to hang in there.

The wombat,[11] who was the smart aleck of the group and had a keen sense of smell, said that Taj should follow his nose.

They became so busy arguing among themselves that they forgot all about Taj, who quietly slipped away.

After this latest round of disappointment, Taj found himself blaming others for his skin problem. All the animals thought they had the answer, but they offered solutions that only made his condition worse. Their voices echoed in Taj's mind and nearly drove him crazy with itch.

He needed to scratch out the noise by finding solitude and silence.

He ran in circles. He ran in lines. But mostly, he tried to run away from himself and his itchy skin.

Until at last, he was utterly lost in the Never

Never Land, with just himself under the sky.

Taj had been so consumed by his need to itch that he hadn't slept or eaten in days. In despair and completely exhausted from nonstop itching, he collapsed noisily to the ground, disturbing Piggi-Billa, the echidna.[12]

Piggi-Billa had dug a burrow beneath the red dirt. She was readying herself for her annual hibernation but scurried to the surface to find out what had caused all the commotion.

Itching, for good reason, isn't something that echidnas do, since their quills make it impossible to scratch their own skin.

But Piggi-Billa had a sharp mind to go with her equally sharp quills. Even though she couldn't relate, she could sense that Taj was filled with grief and despair.

Without a word, she placed herself behind Taj and, ever so gently, began scratching Taj's back with her quills. For the first time in his life, Taj felt some relief, as someone else did the scratching for him. That allowed him to relax, and he finally fell asleep.

When Taj woke up late the next morning, Piggi-Billa was nowhere to be found. As he searched for the echidna, he noticed a glowing red light in the far distance. It seemed to emanate from the ground itself, as if it were the first rays of the morning sunrise.

Having rested, thanks to the echidna, Taj felt a sense of renewed hope, and he had an itch to go investigate the source of the light.

The kindness offered to him by Piggi-Billa gave him the strength that carried him through when he had none left. And with that, he mustered up his newfound strength and made his way across the vast outback toward the glowing red light.

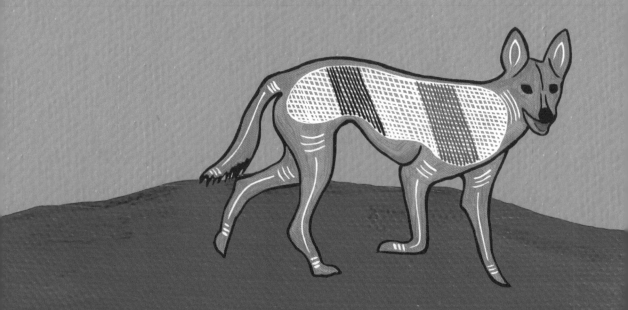

As he got closer, he saw that the red glow was actually the reflection of the sun's rays upon a giant rock. This was Uluru,[13] the island mountain that marks the center of Australia.

Given his weakened state and the many stops he had to make to scratch himself, it took Taj all day to reach Uluru.

By the time he arrived, night had fallen, and the red glow had disappeared into darkness. It was now replaced by a small fire tended by an Original man[14] named You-Know-Me-Before-You-See-Me, a descendant of the First People who had been on this land since time began. He was tasked by the Ancestors to be the keeper and custodian of the surrounding lands.

Exhausted and having lost all hope of ever finding relief from his incessant itching, Taj made up his mind to jump into the flames and end his misery once and for all. He leapt in, but instead of getting burned, the fire went out instantly. He backed away and the fire rekindled.

He tried again, but, just like before, the flames went out. Each time he jumped in, they disappeared, only to reappear when he moved out of range.

He then realized that it was You-Know-Me-Before-You-See-Me who had blown the fire out each time, like candles on a birthday cake.

"Why did he do that?" thought Taj. "What advice could this man offer me?"

You-Know-Me-Before-You-See-Me remained silent, staring intently at the fire while poking it with a stick. While scratching himself, Taj followed his gaze and began noticing familiar scenes within the flames.

In the flames, he could see a dingo running around, meeting bush animals to ask for advice on how to deal with his itching, and doing one silly thing after another, without realizing that each animal's solution only worked for itself!

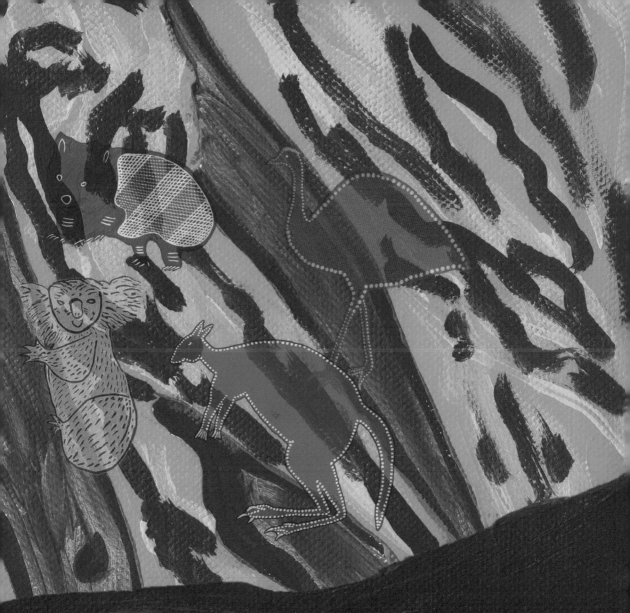

Finally, You-Know-Me-Before-You-See-Me broke his silence. "So, you have the itch to go! Isn't that why they call you a dinGO?" He laughed at his own joke, while the sound "GO" ricocheted against the sandstone walls of Uluru, as if a temple bell had been struck.

As the final echo receded into nothingness, Taj realized that his itching had...gone away with it!

Taj sat without moving for a long time, absorbed in the silence until he heard a rhythmic drone. It came from You-Know-Me-Before-You-See-Me, who had picked up a long, hollow wooden branch called a didgeridoo and started blowing through one end. The sound was so deep and sonorous that it felt as if it was coming from the farthest reaches of Earth itself.

With his ears straight up, Taj listened, transfixed, while up in the sky, the Southern Cross[15] shown brightly above.

Some say that Taj is still there now, free at last.

Facts about Fiction
(for non-Australian readers)

The Itchy Dingo is a story of fiction, but here are real facts, references, and information about some of the characters and inspiration behind the story.

1. Dingoes are as much wolf as they are dogs. They have the ability to rotate their head like an owl and their wrists like humans.

2. Taj was the name of the author's dog, an Australian-born Border Terrier afflicted with an all-consuming itch. This scratching on paper, referred to as a story, is dedicated to his memory.

3. The king brown snake, also known as the Mulga snake, has a bite that delivers a massive amount of venom—enough to fill a shot glass.

4. Kangaroos use their tails to help them balance while jumping.

5. Koalas are very finicky eaters. Their diet consists almost exclusively of eucalyptus leaves, of which they can eat a kilogram a day.

6. The kookaburra is the largest member of the Kingfisher family. Its laughing call sounds like it is having fun at your expense.

7. The platypus has the bill and webbed feet of a duck, the tail of a beaver, the body and fur of an otter, and lays eggs. They are so unique that no one can agree on what the plural of platypus is.

8. A billabong is a waterhole in Australian slang. It is the "pub" where animals meet.

9. The thorny dragon is a lizard covered entirely with conical spines.

10. To "play possum" is to play dead in Australian slang.

11. Wombats are short-legged muscular marsupials with large noses. One of their unusual features is that they poop in cubes.

12. The echidna has spines like a porcupine, a beak like a bird, a pouch like a kangaroo, and lays eggs like a reptile.

13. Uluru is a towering sacred sandstone rock formation in the center of Australia. It is famous for changing color at different times of the day and year, most notably when it glows red at dawn and dusk.

14. The Original Men are the First Australians. Known collectively as Aboriginal Australians, they constitute the longest continuous civilization as descendants of a single founding population that is estimated to have arrived 65,000 years ago. Aboriginal people define themselves as tasked by Ancestors to be the custodians of the land that they inhabit. This sacred connection to the land has allowed for the remarkable diversity of people living in balance and harmony over an entire continent.

DNA analysis conducted by the University of Adelaide made the amazing scientific discovery that no mass movement in response to war over territory, environment changes, or other conflict existed in Australia prior to European arrival in 1788 (Source: Journal of Human Genetics 62, 2016; 343-353).

Imagine if you can: an entire continent where people lived in mutual respect and peace for over a thousand successive generations.

Time will tell if the uncanny coincidence of the brutal removal of Aboriginal people from the lands they were assigned to protect, followed in short order by climate change and its devastating impacts, is mere fiction or fact.

15. The Southern Cross is a kite-shaped group of stars represented in the Australian flag. For Aboriginal people, it marks the head of the "emu in the sky."

About the Author

Patrick Steinemann is an Australian-born multinational whose own itch to travel led him to circle the globe and journey the open road across six continents. The inspiration for this story came while practicing walking meditation at a forest monastery in northern Thailand. He currently resides with his family in Hawaiʻi, where he restores vintage surfboards for art display and surfing.

About the Artist

Michael Connolly, whose Aboriginal name is Mundagutta-Kulliwari, is an artist from Charleville, south-central Queensland, and is a descendent of the Kullilla Tribe on his father's side and the Muruwari People on his mother's side.

Together with his wife, he owns and operates Dreamtime Kullilla Art, an Aboriginal Shop and Gallery.

More information on Dreamtime Kullilla Art can be found at:
http://www.kullillaart.com.au/

CPSIA information can be obtained
at www.ICGtesting.com
Printed in the USA
BVHW022021120922
646859BV00002B/18